# Success-Speak
## The Art of Maximizing Your Potential Through What You Say

# *Journal*

*A Full Year of Inspiring Success Quotes from*

# Steven K. Dunn

THREE SKILLET

SUCCESS-SPEAK: THE ART OF MAXIMIZING YOUR POTENTIAL
THROUGH WHAT YOU SAY, JOURNAL EDITION, Dunn, Steven K.

1st ed.

◆◉◆ THREE SKILLET

www.ThreeSkilletPublishing.com

ISBN: 978-1-943189-49-6

# — Introduction —

C. S. Lewis once said that a man can no more diminish God's glory by refusing to worship Him than a lunatic can put out the sun by scribbling the word "darkness" on the walls of his cell.

Finding success in everyday life is the same for many of us. People around us are constantly scribbling disparaging frowns, snide comments, and gut-busting criticisms on our attempts to rise above our circumstances.

We can escape their prison cells with *Success-Speak*. We can recharge our minds and bask in the sunlight of success by saying these three words: *I will succeed.*

Of course, it's more difficult than just saying three words, but that's a good place to start. Once we've internalized that concept, we can move on into specific areas of our life where we can begin to see results. Soon we'll keep the sink clean every day. We'll get dressed before we get the mail. We'll register for that college class, apply for that job; and we'll get there, even if we must beg a ride.

You see, success happens because we make it happen. No one in the prison cell of defeat has the right to tell us our success can't happen, all because they've written our future on the wall. Our future isn't in their hands. It's in ours.

This book gives you *Success-Speak* jump starters for every day of the year. Read them first thing in the morning to get your mind on how you are going to make your day successful. Then *write it down.* You're making a plan and setting a goal for the day. You are saying, "This is how I'm changing my life from this day forward. This is the new me, not the writing on yesterday's wall. My prison cell of defeat can't hold me any longer. I've left that building, the doors are locked, and I can't get back inside. I'm moving forward into my new life."

If you want to find success in your life, *Success-Speak* will help you get there. Your job is to take the first step with Day 1.

Let's get started.

Steven K. Dunn
Author of *Success Speak: The Art of Maximizing Your Potential Through What You Say*

"If you don't shake off your doubts and forge a path forward through the veiled path of possibilities and unknowns before you, then you will never know what heights you can reach, the dreams you can accomplish, or the positive difference you can impart."

—— Steven K. Dunn ——

# — Day 1 —

*"If you let your personal life, your family, or your spirituality suffer to further wealth or power, then you have not been successful."*

◄ *My Words of Success for Today* ►

_____

_____

_____

_____

_____

_____

_____

_____

_____

_____

# — Day 2 —

*"Even the greatest accomplishments in our life are eclipsed by the glory of God. Serve Him in all that you do."*

*◄ My Words of Success for Today ►*

_____

_____

_____

_____

_____

_____

_____

_____

_____

## — Day 3 —

*"If you make an attempt and don't succeed, that is not a failure. All you've done is discovered one way not to proceed. Get up, learn from your experience, and make another attempt."*

◀ *My Words of Success for Today* ▶

_____

_____

_____

_____

_____

_____

_____

_____

_____

# — Day 4 —

*"Nearly all of us know the pain that comes with being deceived. Yet even knowing that, are you still going to tell that lie?"*

◀ *My Words of Success for Today* ▶

_____

_____

_____

_____

_____

_____

_____

_____

_____

# — Day 5 —

*"If you cannot stand by your actions without feeling ashamed, then the time to change is now."*

◄ *My Words of Success for Today* ►

_____

_____

_____

_____

_____

_____

_____

_____

_____

# — Day 6 —

*"If you want success, then you can achieve it."*

◀ *My Words of Success for Today* ▶

_____

_____

_____

_____

_____

_____

_____

_____

_____

_____

# — Day 7 —

*"Success is not something that comes
without significant work."*

◄ *My Words of Success for Today* ►

_____

_____

_____

_____

_____

_____

_____

_____

_____

# — Day 8 —

*"Holding grudges will hold you back in life."*

◄ *My Words of Success for Today* ►

_____

_____

_____

_____

_____

_____

_____

_____

_____

_____

# — Day 9 —

*"If you truly want to achieve your goal, to live your dreams, you will not let anything stand in your path."*

◄ *My Words of Success for Today* ►

_____

_____

_____

_____

_____

_____

_____

_____

_____

_____

# — Day 10 —

*"Remember that success rarely falls into your lap, for you must make the conscious decision to succeed before success can be yours."*

◄ *My Words of Success for Today* ►

_____

_____

_____

_____

_____

_____

_____

_____

_____

_____

# — Day 11 —

*"A single action can resonate throughout your entire life, whether it be negative or positive."*

◄ *My Words of Success for Today* ►

_____

_____

_____

_____

_____

_____

_____

_____

_____

_____

# — Day 12 —

*"Conflict is not always the answer."*

◂ *My Words of Success for Today* ▸

_____

_____

_____

_____

_____

_____

_____

_____

_____

_____

# — Day 13 —

*"Adapt. It is something that must be done constantly to be able to succeed in the world."*

◀ *My Words of Success for Today* ▶

_____

_____

_____

_____

_____

_____

_____

_____

_____

# — Day 14 —

*"Always seek to push yourself to new heights."*

*◄ My Words of Success for Today ►*

_____

_____

_____

_____

_____

_____

_____

_____

_____

_____

# — Day 15 —

*"The knowledge that you learn from making the wrong decision can often be just as valuable as the knowledge you learn from making the right decision."*

◄ *My Words of Success for Today* ►

_____

_____

_____

_____

_____

_____

_____

_____

_____

# — Day 16 —

*"To dwell on your regrets is to be lodged
in the past."*

◀ *My Words of Success for Today* ▶

_____

_____

_____

_____

_____

_____

_____

_____

_____

_____

# — Day 17 —

*"The path of success is not idle time and waiting. The path to success is that of hard work and persistence."*

◂ *My Words of Success for Today* ▸

---

---

---

---

---

---

---

---

---

# — Day 18 —

*"Take a step back, look at your life, decide what could be improved, and work every single day at achieving your goal."*

◂ *My Words of Success for Today* ▸

_____

_____

_____

_____

_____

_____

_____

_____

_____

## — Day 19 —

*"Once you let your desire for greater success turn into greed, you are stunting your ability to reach your full potential."*

◀ *My Words of Success for Today* ▶

_____

_____

_____

_____

_____

_____

_____

_____

_____

_____

# — Day 20 —

*"Watch closely, for if you can learn from the mistakes of others, then you can prevent yourself from making the same errors."*

◄ *My Words of Success for Today* ►

_____

_____

_____

_____

_____

_____

_____

_____

_____

# — Day 21 —

*"Whether it be today or in 20 years, you will always face the consequences of your actions."*

◀ *My Words of Success for Today* ▶

_____

_____

_____

_____

_____

_____

_____

_____

_____

# — Day 22 —

*"Do not let a failure shake your foundation."*

◄ *My Words of Success for Today* ►

_____

_____

_____

_____

_____

_____

_____

_____

_____

_____

# — Day 23 —

*"Do you just want to be happy or to
actually make a difference in this world?"*

◀ *My Words of Success for Today* ▶

_____

_____

_____

_____

_____

_____

_____

_____

_____

# — Day 24 —

*"To truly be successful in the fullest sense of the word, you must succeed in all aspects of life . . . not just one."*

◀ *My Words of Success for Today* ▶

_____

_____

_____

_____

_____

_____

_____

_____

_____

_____

# — Day 25 —

*"Who will you be? You can either be the one watching the world change around you or you can be the one changing the world. It's time to make a choice."*

◄ *My Words of Success for Today* ►

_____

_____

_____

_____

_____

_____

_____

_____

_____

_____

# — Day 26 —

*"Even the person who walks straight and true for his entire life will have made mistakes, fallen, and damaged the lives of others inadvertently. Apologize and move on."*

◄ *My Words of Success for Today* ►

_____

_____

_____

_____

_____

_____

_____

_____

_____

_____

# — Day 27 —

*"A single word or action can bring down
the mightiest and devastate someone
emotionally and physically. Choose your
words and actions with care."*

◂ *My Words of Success for Today* ▸

_____

_____

_____

_____

_____

_____

_____

_____

_____

_____

# — Day 28 —

*"Do you like what you see around yourself? Do you want things to be different? Then change them. Yes, bringing about change is that simple."*

◀ *My Words of Success for Today* ▶

---

---

---

---

---

---

---

---

---

# — Day 29 —

*"You must be the one to make the choice
to become successful."*

◀ *My Words of Success for Today* ▶

_____

_____

_____

_____

_____

_____

_____

_____

_____

_____

# — Day 30 —

*"Success requires persistence during the worst of times."*

_____

_____

_____

_____

_____

_____

_____

_____

_____

# — Day 31 —

*"If you are lodged in the past, then the future will slip past you and along with it your chances for success."*

◀ *My Words of Success for Today* ▶

_____

_____

_____

_____

_____

_____

_____

_____

_____

# — Day 32 —

*"Have you told Jesus 'thank you' today? If not, you should do so right now."*

◄ *My Words of Success for Today* ►

_____

_____

_____

_____

_____

_____

_____

_____

_____

_____

# — Day 33 —

*"Learn about the world around you.*
*Observe it, study its history, and*
*understand the mistakes it has made.*
*Only then can you truly make progress."*

◀ *My Words of Success for Today* ▶

_____

_____

_____

_____

_____

_____

_____

_____

_____

_____

# — Day 34 —

*"Even if you seek perfection, to cause no harm, or to just do all the good you can achieve, know that the success will still come bound with occasional failures."*

_____

_____

_____

_____

_____

_____

_____

_____

_____

_____

# — Day 35 —

*"Your greatest strength comes when you turn loose of your reservations."*

◄ *My Words of Success for Today* ►

_____

_____

_____

_____

_____

_____

_____

_____

_____

# — Day 36 —

*"Do not fear living your life to its greatest potential."*

◄ *My Words of Success for Today* ►

---

---

---

---

---

---

---

---

---

---

# — Day 37 —

*"There is only one person on this earth with the power to prevent you from reaching your full potential and achieving success beyond your wildest dreams. That person is you!"*

◀ *My Words of Success for Today* ▶

_____

_____

_____

_____

_____

_____

_____

_____

_____

_____

# — Day 38 —

*"Don't let your chance for success slip away just because the path becomes rocky."*

◄ *My Words of Success for Today* ►

_____

_____

_____

_____

_____

_____

_____

_____

_____

# — Day 39 —

*"If you don't know what to do, then it may be time for you to find yourself a role model."*

◄ *My Words of Success for Today* ►

_____

_____

_____

_____

_____

_____

_____

_____

_____

_____

# — Day 40 —

*"You can overcome any obstacle."*

*◄ My Words of Success for Today ►*

_____

_____

_____

_____

_____

_____

_____

_____

_____

# — Day 41 —

*"You must surmount the obstructions in your path if you truly desire to succeed."*

◀ *My Words of Success for Today* ▶

_____

_____

_____

_____

_____

_____

_____

_____

_____

_____

# — Day 42 —

*"It's not the obstacles in your life that determine who you are; it's your decisions."*

◄ *My Words of Success for Today* ►

_____

_____

_____

_____

_____

_____

_____

_____

_____

_____

# — Day 43 —

*"Act on every good opportunity. Make
your move now."*

◀ *My Words of Success for Today* ▶

_____

_____

_____

_____

_____

_____

_____

_____

_____

# — Day 44 —

*"Do not let yourself be defeated by something as simple as a lack of faith."*

◄ *My Words of Success for Today* ►

_____

_____

_____

_____

_____

_____

_____

_____

_____

# — Day 45 —

*"You need to be cautious to not lose your moral base, the foundation that is who you are."*

◀ *My Words of Success for Today* ▶

_____

_____

_____

_____

_____

_____

_____

_____

_____

# — Day 46 —

*"Balance your desire for advancement with wisdom. An overstep can cost you everything."*

◁ *My Words of Success for Today* ▷

_____

_____

_____

_____

_____

_____

_____

_____

_____

_____

# — Day 47 —

*"Some things can only truly be understood through experiencing them yourself."*

_____

_____

_____

_____

_____

_____

_____

_____

_____

# — Day 48 —

*"Move on, overcome, and know that your
past is not the future."*

◄ *My Words of Success for Today* ►

_____

_____

_____

_____

_____

_____

_____

_____

_____

_____

# — Day 49 —

*"It isn't until you have lost everything,*
*that you truly know what you had."*

_____

_____

_____

_____

_____

_____

_____

_____

_____

_____

# — Day 50 —

*"Don't ever stand still. You must be moving forward and reaching for your goals."*

◄ *My Words of Success for Today* ►

_____

_____

_____

_____

_____

_____

_____

_____

_____

_____

# — Day 51 —

*"Always walk forward, never backwards."*

◀ *My Words of Success for Today* ▶

_____

_____

_____

_____

_____

_____

_____

_____

_____

# — Day 52 —

*"Seeing and believing are two very different things."*

◂ *My Words of Success for Today* ▸

_____

_____

_____

_____

_____

_____

_____

_____

_____

_____

# — Day 53 —

*"Not all battles are worth fighting."*

*◄ My Words of Success for Today ►*

_____

_____

_____

_____

_____

_____

_____

_____

_____

_____

# — Day 54 —

*"Let your past experiences strengthen you for the future."*

◄ *My Words of Success for Today* ►

_____

_____

_____

_____

_____

_____

_____

_____

_____

_____

# — Day 55 —

*"Every failed attempt is an opportunity to learn."*

◁ *My Words of Success for Today* ▷

_____

_____

_____

_____

_____

_____

_____

_____

_____

# — Day 56 —

*"The direction taken is often more dependent upon someone's views rather than the actual facts."*

◀ *My Words of Success for Today* ▶

_____

_____

_____

_____

_____

_____

_____

_____

_____

# — Day 57 —

*"Impatience results in mistakes just as accidents cause death."*

◀ *My Words of Success for Today* ▶

_____

_____

_____

_____

_____

_____

_____

_____

_____

_____

# — Day 58 —

*"Is the cost worth the gain? That is a question you must ask yourself for everything you want."*

_____

_____

_____

_____

_____

_____

_____

_____

_____

_____

# — Day 59 —

*"How well you have succeeded is determined not only by what has been achieved, but how you handled the failures."*

◀ *My Words of Success for Today* ▶

_____

_____

_____

_____

_____

_____

_____

_____

_____

_____

# — Day 60 —

*"Don't fear what you don't know. It's the unknown that brings forth greatness, achievement, and more importantly, success."*

◀ *My Words of Success for Today* ▶

_____

_____

_____

_____

_____

_____

_____

_____

_____

_____

# — Day 61 —

*"Once your doubts are overcome, there will be no stopping you."*

◄ *My Words of Success for Today* ►

_____

_____

_____

_____

_____

_____

_____

_____

_____

_____

# — Day 62 —

*"If you stray from the path of what is right, don't surrender; you must stand up and step back onto the path of that which is worthwhile and righteous."*

◄ *My Words of Success for Today* ►

_____

_____

_____

_____

_____

_____

_____

_____

_____

# — Day 63 —

*"If you do not have the mental attitude of success and the faith to persevere, then your potential will go unfulfilled."*

◁ *My Words of Success for Today* ▷

_____

_____

_____

_____

_____

_____

_____

_____

_____

_____

# — Day 64 —

*"Just because you are victorious doesn't mean you are the winner. Were the sacrifices to achieve the victory worth the cost?"*

◀ *My Words of Success for Today* ▶

_____

_____

_____

_____

_____

_____

_____

_____

_____

_____

# — Day 65 —

*"Find somebody you can look up to. Take
a look at their life, how they failed and
succeeded.  Take that knowledge and use
it create your own success."*

◂ *My Words of Success for Today* ▸

_____

_____

_____

_____

_____

_____

_____

_____

_____

# — Day 66 —

*"Know who you were, know who you are, and most importantly, know who you want to be."*

_____

_____

_____

_____

_____

_____

_____

_____

_____

# — Day 67 —

*"It's how you handle the challenges you face that define you."*

◀ *My Words of Success for Today* ▶

_____

_____

_____

_____

_____

_____

_____

_____

_____

_____

# — Day 68 —

*"It isn't whether something's actually possible, as all things are possible. It's whether you believe that it's possible."*

_____

_____

_____

_____

_____

_____

_____

_____

_____

_____

# — Day 69 —

*"Don't let yourself get too deeply embedded in events. It is wise to stop, take a step back, and see the complete picture."*

◀ *My Words of Success for Today* ▶

_____

_____

_____

_____

_____

_____

_____

_____

_____

_____

# — Day 70 —

*"The first step to improving your life is setting the goal of who you want to be."*

◀ *My Words of Success for Today* ▶

_____

_____

_____

_____

_____

_____

_____

_____

_____

# — Day 71 —

*"Don't expect rational actions from irrational people."*

◁ *My Words of Success for Today* ▷

_____

_____

_____

_____

_____

_____

_____

_____

_____

# — Day 72 —

*"Always remember to keep your priorities in check. All it takes is forgetting once what comes first in your life to lose all that is dear to you."*

◀ *My Words of Success for Today* ▶

_____

_____

_____

_____

_____

_____

_____

_____

_____

# — Day 73 —

*"The greatest opposition to success will be
your own inhibitions and doubts."*

◂ *My Words of Success for Today* ▸

_____

_____

_____

_____

_____

_____

_____

_____

_____

_____

# — Day 74 —

*"Don't let anger consume you; all it will do is take you to a place that you don't want to go."*

◁ *My Words of Success for Today* ▷

_____

_____

_____

_____

_____

_____

_____

_____

_____

_____

# — Day 75 —

*"Don't act hastily or your path will be wrought with mistakes."*

◄ *My Words of Success for Today* ►

_____

_____

_____

_____

_____

_____

_____

_____

_____

_____

# — Day 76 —

*"There is always a choice."*

◀ *My Words of Success for Today* ▶

_____

_____

_____

_____

_____

_____

_____

_____

_____

# — Day 77 —

*"Fight only the battles that are going to
make a substantive difference."*

◄ *My Words of Success for Today* ►

_____

_____

_____

_____

_____

_____

_____

_____

_____

_____

# — Day 78 —

*"Learn at least one new thing every day. Always continue to expand your knowledge."*

◄ *My Words of Success for Today* ►

_____

_____

_____

_____

_____

_____

_____

_____

_____

# — Day 79 —

*"There is no excuse for not moving forward in life."*

*◄ My Words of Success for Today ►*

_____

_____

_____

_____

_____

_____

_____

_____

_____

_____

# — Day 80 —

*"If you see and do nothing, you have chosen not to act. The responsibility is yours."*

◄ *My Words of Success for Today* ►

_____

_____

_____

_____

_____

_____

_____

_____

_____

# — Day 81 —

*"You have a choice in life. You can either run or you can overcome what you fear."*

◁ *My Words of Success for Today* ▷

_____

_____

_____

_____

_____

_____

_____

_____

_____

# — Day 82 —

*"You must remember that for every new thing you acquire, a price will be paid, whether it be money, time, or relationships."*

◀ *My Words of Success for Today* ▶

_____

_____

_____

_____

_____

_____

_____

_____

_____

# — Day 83 —

*"Stand tall, walk straight, and be unafraid."*

◄ *My Words of Success for Today* ►

_____

_____

_____

_____

_____

_____

_____

_____

_____

_____

# — Day 84 —

*"A choice stands before you. You can either sit idly by while the world changes and have no control. Or you can make a stand and be the one changing the world."*

◄ *My Words of Success for Today* ►

_____

_____

_____

_____

_____

_____

_____

_____

_____

_____

# — Day 85 —

*"Success comes from hard work, faith, and the confidence to utilize the opportunities that come across your path."*

◄ *My Words of Success for Today* ►

_____

_____

_____

_____

_____

_____

_____

_____

_____

_____

# — Day 86 —

*"What do you really want out of life? Is it really just financial success, or is it happiness—the satisfaction and joy of a complete life?"*

◁ *My Words of Success for Today* ▷

_____

_____

_____

_____

_____

_____

_____

_____

_____

# — Day 87 —

*"Listen to the advice of those around you, but take to heart what your instincts tell you to do."*

◄ *My Words of Success for Today* ►

_____

_____

_____

_____

_____

_____

_____

_____

_____

_____

# — Day 88 —

*"Asking for help is not a sign of weakness;
it's a sign of wisdom."*

◂ *My Words of Success for Today* ▸

_____

_____

_____

_____

_____

_____

_____

_____

_____

# — Day 89 —

*"Any goal, any objective is possible . . . at a cost."*

_____

_____

_____

_____

_____

_____

_____

_____

_____

_____

# — Day 90 —

*"Do not let your fear of loss inhibit your
ability to succeed."*

*◄ My Words of Success for Today ►*

_____

_____

_____

_____

_____

_____

_____

_____

_____

# — Day 91 —

*"Your primary path to failure is to give in to defeat."*

_____

_____

_____

_____

_____

_____

_____

_____

_____

# — Day 92 —

*"Seek and hold onto the living Word of God with all your strength."*

◁ *My Words of Success for Today* ▷

_____

_____

_____

_____

_____

_____

_____

_____

_____

_____

# — Day 93 —

*"Your understanding is limited by what
you allow it to be."*

◄ *My Words of Success for Today* ►

_____

_____

_____

_____

_____

_____

_____

_____

_____

# — Day 94 —

*"Set a goal today, one that is further than
you have ever achieved before."*

◁ *My Words of Success for Today* ▷

_____

_____

_____

_____

_____

_____

_____

_____

_____

_____

# — Day 95 —

*"Understand that you may not be the only person attempting to achieve your goals. Act soon before the opportunity goes to someone else."*

◂ *My Words of Success for Today* ▸

_____

_____

_____

_____

_____

_____

_____

_____

_____

_____

# — Day 96 —

*"Don't let fear stand in the way of
achieving your potential."*

◁ *My Words of Success for Today* ▷

_____

_____

_____

_____

_____

_____

_____

_____

_____

_____

# — Day 97 —

*"Don't falter when obstacles appear in your path. With perseverance, they will be overcome and success will be yours."*

◄ *My Words of Success for Today* ►

_____

_____

_____

_____

_____

_____

_____

_____

_____

# — Day 98 —

*"Don't let regret hold you back from the future you can have or the success you can achieve."*

◀ *My Words of Success for Today* ▶

_____

_____

_____

_____

_____

_____

_____

_____

_____

# — Day 99 —

*"Don't let tomorrow be the same as today. Reach out, push forward, and make progress."*

◄ *My Words of Success for Today* ►

_____

_____

_____

_____

_____

_____

_____

_____

_____

_____

# — Day 100 —

*"How you choose to spend your time is a
key definition of your character."*

◄ *My Words of Success for Today* ►

_____

_____

_____

_____

_____

_____

_____

_____

_____

_____

# — Day 101 —

*"Continually increasing your knowledge equates to the furthering and expanding of the horizons before you."*

◄ *My Words of Success for Today* ►

_____

_____

_____

_____

_____

_____

_____

_____

_____

# — Day 102 —

*"Without the belief that you can achieve your goals, it is unlikely that you ever will."*

◀ *My Words of Success for Today* ▶

_____

_____

_____

_____

_____

_____

_____

_____

_____

# — Day 103 —

*"Seek out not how to win but how to succeed."*

◀ *My Words of Success for Today* ▶

_____

_____

_____

_____

_____

_____

_____

_____

_____

# — Day 104 —

*"You must believe in your success."*

*◄ My Words of Success for Today ►*

_____

_____

_____

_____

_____

_____

_____

_____

_____

_____

# — Day 105 —

*"Preparation is key to achieving your goals and being successful."*

◄ *My Words of Success for Today* ►

_____

_____

_____

_____

_____

_____

_____

_____

_____

# — Day 106 —

*"Neither fear nor bravado is always the
correct choice, and wisdom is to know
when to flee or to hold your ground."*

◀ *My Words of Success for Today* ▶

_____

_____

_____

_____

_____

_____

_____

_____

_____

# — Day 107 —

*"Understand the past, but do not dwell in it."*

◀ *My Words of Success for Today* ▶

_____

_____

_____

_____

_____

_____

_____

_____

_____

_____

# — Day 108 —

*"Much may stand in your path, but if you allow success to be your only option, then success you will find."*

◄ *My Words of Success for Today* ►

_____

_____

_____

_____

_____

_____

_____

_____

_____

# — Day 109 —

*"You can be the one shaping the world;*
*you just can't let fear stand in your way."*

_____

_____

_____

_____

_____

_____

_____

_____

_____

# — Day 110 —

*"The choice to be successful is yours and not based upon where you grew up, your education, your life previous to this point, or who people say you are."*

◁ *My Words of Success for Today* ▷

_____

_____

_____

_____

_____

_____

_____

_____

_____

# — Day 111 —

*"One person's version of success may not be the same as yours. Ask yourself what you really desire."*

_____

_____

_____

_____

_____

_____

_____

_____

_____

## — Day 112 —

*"Make the choice that you know is the correct decision and not just what people tell you is right."*

_____

_____

_____

_____

_____

_____

_____

_____

_____

_____

# — Day 113 —

*"Don't let excuses stand in your way of success."*

◀ *My Words of Success for Today* ▶

_____

_____

_____

_____

_____

_____

_____

_____

_____

# — Day 114 —

*"Before committing your life to a goal or objective, you need to ensure that the cost is worth the gain."*

◄ *My Words of Success for Today* ►

_____

_____

_____

_____

_____

_____

_____

_____

_____

_____

# — Day 115 —

*"It isn't what the mistake was or how you made it, but instead how you recovered from that mistake and what you've learned from the experience."*

◂ *My Words of Success for Today* ▸

_____

_____

_____

_____

_____

_____

_____

_____

_____

# — Day 116 —

*"As long as you are moving forward, failure should never be a word in your vocabulary."*

◄ *My Words of Success for Today* ►

_____

_____

_____

_____

_____

_____

_____

_____

_____

_____

## — Day 117 —

*"The strength to succeed is multiplied when you have faith in your success to accomplish your goals."*

◀ *My Words of Success for Today* ▶

_____

_____

_____

_____

_____

_____

_____

_____

_____

_____

# — Day 118 —

*"Be brave, stand by all that you've done,
and don't hide from what you can
become."*

◄ *My Words of Success for Today* ►

_____

_____

_____

_____

_____

_____

_____

_____

_____

# — Day 119 —

*"Today, create and formulate a plan to achieve at least one goal."*

◀ *My Words of Success for Today* ▶

_____

_____

_____

_____

_____

_____

_____

_____

_____

# — Day 120 —

*"If you desire change, then you must be
the one to take hold of it and lead it into
the open."*

◀ *My Words of Success for Today* ▶

_____

_____

_____

_____

_____

_____

_____

_____

_____

_____

## — Day 121 —

*"There's a difference between what's within your perceived grasp and what is actually within your reach. Don't let yourself be held back."*

◄ My Words of Success for Today ►

_____

_____

_____

_____

_____

_____

_____

_____

_____

# — Day 122 —

*"The greatest achievements are those that
you accomplish for the Lord."*

◄ *My Words of Success for Today* ►

_____

_____

_____

_____

_____

_____

_____

_____

_____

_____

# — Day 123 —

*"You must have a specific goal if you don't want to waste your time and energy reaching for success."*

◀ *My Words of Success for Today* ▶

_____

_____

_____

_____

_____

_____

_____

_____

_____

# — Day 124 —

*"Make a goal and don't surrender it."*

◂ *My Words of Success for Today* ▸

_____

_____

_____

_____

_____

_____

_____

_____

_____

_____

# — Day 125 —

*"Don't let the past prevent you from achieving your potential in the future."*

◀ *My Words of Success for Today* ▶

_____

_____

_____

_____

_____

_____

_____

_____

_____

# — Day 126 —

*"Commitment is required to achieve your goals."*

◄ *My Words of Success for Today* ►

_____

_____

_____

_____

_____

_____

_____

_____

_____

# — Day 127 —

*"If you can't stand proudly by all that you've done, then it's time to make a difference in how you live your life."*

◄ *My Words of Success for Today* ►

_____

_____

_____

_____

_____

_____

_____

_____

_____

# — Day 128 —

*"Do not act rashly; for with such actions come mistakes."*

*◄ My Words of Success for Today ►*

_____

_____

_____

_____

_____

_____

_____

_____

_____

# — Day 129 —

*"To instigate change we must act on what we know is right."*

◀ *My Words of Success for Today* ▶

_____

_____

_____

_____

_____

_____

_____

_____

_____

# — Day 130 —

*"Understand, learn, and continue forward."*

◄ *My Words of Success for Today* ►

_____

_____

_____

_____

_____

_____

_____

_____

_____

# — Day 131 —

*"Being patient will change your life in a profound way."*

◄ *My Words of Success for Today* ►

_____

_____

_____

_____

_____

_____

_____

_____

_____

# — Day 132 —

*"Success is measured not by how far you traveled, but instead by how well you traveled."*

◀ *My Words of Success for Today* ▶

---

---

---

---

---

---

---

---

---

# — Day 133 —

*"Success is solely based upon whether you make the choice to succeed and are willing to make the necessary sacrifices to achieve success."*

◀ *My Words of Success for Today* ▶

_____

_____

_____

_____

_____

_____

_____

_____

_____

_____

# — Day 134 —

*"Show the path to those who need to see it. Those that are wandering, lost, and without direction need assistance to get their life together and to begin making advancements."*

◄ *My Words of Success for Today* ►

_____

_____

_____

_____

_____

_____

_____

_____

_____

## — Day 135 —

*"Watch out for the fallacies of others and their personal agendas. Just remember that the choice is yours to make, and the responsibility from that decision is yours as well."*

◀ *My Words of Success for Today* ▶

_____

_____

_____

_____

_____

_____

_____

_____

_____

# — Day 136 —

*"Every excuse you make is one step backwards from your goal."*

◀ *My Words of Success for Today* ▶

_____

_____

_____

_____

_____

_____

_____

_____

_____

_____

# — Day 137 —

*"Take a look at your goal, what you desire,
and ask yourself what the price of success
is and if it is worth the cost, not only to
yourself, but to those around you, as well."*

◀ *My Words of Success for Today* ▶

_____

_____

_____

_____

_____

_____

_____

_____

_____

# — Day 138 —

*"Never underestimate the task at hand or
the obstacles in your path. Success
requires determination and attention."*

◀ *My Words of Success for Today* ▶

_____

_____

_____

_____

_____

_____

_____

_____

_____

_____

# — Day 139 —

*"Don't fear what you may face, for you have the capability to overcome any obstacle in your path."*

◀ *My Words of Success for Today* ▶

_____

_____

_____

_____

_____

_____

_____

_____

_____

# — Day 140 —

*"Defend your beliefs, fight for your desires, but never stand still."*

◀ *My Words of Success for Today* ▶

_____

_____

_____

_____

_____

_____

_____

_____

_____

# — Day 141 —

*"Holding a grudge is like picking up a hot stone. It burns the hand that touches it."*

◂ *My Words of Success for Today* ▸

_____

_____

_____

_____

_____

_____

_____

_____

_____

# — Day 142 —

*"Always and continually seek to improve yourself."*

*◀ My Words of Success for Today ▶*

_____

_____

_____

_____

_____

_____

_____

_____

_____

_____

# — Day 143 —

*"Remember to lead by example, as that is often the most influential manner to instigate change."*

◀ *My Words of Success for Today* ▶

_____

_____

_____

_____

_____

_____

_____

_____

_____

# — Day 144 —

*"There are those who would seek to derail you from your path. Stay steadfast, and you will not fail to reach your goal."*

◀ *My Words of Success for Today* ▶

_____

_____

_____

_____

_____

_____

_____

_____

_____

# — Day 145 —

*"You must work diligently and with perseverance to succeed."*

◁ *My Words of Success for Today* ▷

_____

_____

_____

_____

_____

_____

_____

_____

_____

# — Day 146 —

*"Do not fear the unknown; for from the unknown some of your greatest gifts and achievements will come."*

◀ *My Words of Success for Today* ▶

_____

_____

_____

_____

_____

_____

_____

_____

_____

# — Day 147 —

*"To achieve great things, you must first have faith that they are possible."*

◀ *My Words of Success for Today* ▶

_____

_____

_____

_____

_____

_____

_____

_____

_____

_____

# — Day 148 —

*"No amount of plans will ever change your life without your actions to back them up!"*

◀ *My Words of Success for Today* ▶

_____

_____

_____

_____

_____

_____

_____

_____

_____

_____

# — Day 149 —

*"If something negatively influences your life, then change what is negatively influencing you. If you can't change it, get rid of it."*

◀ *My Words of Success for Today* ▶

_____

_____

_____

_____

_____

_____

_____

_____

_____

# — Day 150 —

*"With faith in your success, you are
already on the correct path."*

◄ *My Words of Success for Today* ►

_____

_____

_____

_____

_____

_____

_____

_____

_____

# — Day 151 —

*"Those who act are the ones who will
make a positive difference in the world."*

◄ *My Words of Success for Today* ►

_____

_____

_____

_____

_____

_____

_____

_____

_____

# — Day 152 —

*"The most important thing you can do to achieve success is serve the LORD with your entire heart."*

◄ *My Words of Success for Today* ►

_____

_____

_____

_____

_____

_____

_____

_____

_____

# — Day 153 —

*"Do not feel rushed, for it will only cause you to make mistakes."*

◄ *My Words of Success for Today* ►

_____

_____

_____

_____

_____

_____

_____

_____

_____

# — Day 154 —

*"It is far better to do things correctly the first time, rather than repeat the process several times to get it correct."*

◀ *My Words of Success for Today* ▶

_____

_____

_____

_____

_____

_____

_____

_____

_____

## — Day 155 —

*"Believing that success will be yours is only the first step. Before it can become a reality, you must also act on your belief."*

_____

_____

_____

_____

_____

_____

_____

_____

_____

_____

# — Day 156 —

*"The potential for success is within you.*
*It's time to make the choice."*

◀ *My Words of Success for Today* ▶

_____

_____

_____

_____

_____

_____

_____

_____

_____

_____

# — Day 157 —

*"All it usually takes is to show people that there's a path available, and that path will lead to an improvement of people's lives."*

_____

_____

_____

_____

_____

_____

_____

_____

_____

# — Day 158 —

*"There are always risks on your path to achieve your goals."*

◄ *My Words of Success for Today* ►

_____

_____

_____

_____

_____

_____

_____

_____

_____

# — Day 159 —

*"You have a choice. You can either make excuses for yourself and your actions, or you can achieve success. You can't do both."*

_____

_____

_____

_____

_____

_____

_____

_____

_____

_____

# — Day 160 —

*"You can't be afraid of hard work if you desire success."*

◀ *My Words of Success for Today* ▶

_____

_____

_____

_____

_____

_____

_____

_____

_____

_____

# — Day 161 —

*"It may feel as if all your options have closed before you, but you are only lost if you stop walking forward."*

◀ *My Words of Success for Today* ▶

_____

_____

_____

_____

_____

_____

_____

_____

_____

_____

# — Day 162 —

*"Don't fear losing what you never had in the first place."*

◀ *My Words of Success for Today* ▶

_____

_____

_____

_____

_____

_____

_____

_____

_____

_____

# — Day 163 —

*"Forgiveness is the only choice if you want
to move forward in your life."*

◄ *My Words of Success for Today* ►

_____

_____

_____

_____

_____

_____

_____

_____

_____

_____

# — Day 164 —

*"You have a choice. You can either cower
in the corner or overcome those who
would seek to destroy you."*

◄ *My Words of Success for Today* ►

_____

_____

_____

_____

_____

_____

_____

_____

_____

_____

# — Day 165 —

*"If you never stop learning and growing, then you will continually be achieving greater levels of success."*

◄ *My Words of Success for Today* ►

_____

_____

_____

_____

_____

_____

_____

_____

_____

_____

# — Day 166 —

*"Dwelling in the past will not allow you to make progress towards the future."*

◄ *My Words of Success for Today* ►

_____

_____

_____

_____

_____

_____

_____

_____

_____

# — Day 167 —

*"Knowledge is a bringer of success."*

◀ *My Words of Success for Today* ▶

_____

_____

_____

_____

_____

_____

_____

_____

_____

# — Day 168 —

*"Don't let one failure get you down . . . or the next hundred."*

_____

_____

_____

_____

_____

_____

_____

_____

_____

# — Day 169 —

*"Success does not come easily. It requires hard work, patience, and the will to persist in your effort to succeed."*

◀ *My Words of Success for Today* ▶

_____

_____

_____

_____

_____

_____

_____

_____

_____

_____

# — Day 170 —

*"Success rarely falls into your lap; you must make the conscious decision to succeed before it can be yours."*

◀ *My Words of Success for Today* ▶

_____

_____

_____

_____

_____

_____

_____

_____

_____

_____

# — Day 171 —

*"Those you associate with will leave a
lasting impression on you."*

_____

_____

_____

_____

_____

_____

_____

_____

_____

_____

# — Day 172 —

*"Each day you move forward you are progressing towards true success."*

◀ *My Words of Success for Today* ▶

_____

_____

_____

_____

_____

_____

_____

_____

_____

# — Day 173 —

*"Just because somebody understands what they need to do doesn't mean that they know how to do it."*

◀ *My Words of Success for Today* ▶

_____

_____

_____

_____

_____

_____

_____

_____

_____

# — Day 174 —

*"You can be part of those who will change the world, but you must be willing to do what you know is right."*

◀ *My Words of Success for Today* ▶

_____

_____

_____

_____

_____

_____

_____

_____

_____

## — Day 175 —

*"Do not regret your mistakes. Understand how you made the mistake, find a solution to prevent it from occurring again, and take heart in the knowledge that you have improved."*

◂ *My Words of Success for Today* ▸

_____

_____

_____

_____

_____

_____

_____

_____

_____

# — Day 176 —

*"Having patience will allow you to complete your tasks far more efficiently."*

*◄ My Words of Success for Today ►*

_____

_____

_____

_____

_____

_____

_____

_____

_____

# — Day 177 —

*"Take responsibility for your actions."*

◄ *My Words of Success for Today* ►

_____

_____

_____

_____

_____

_____

_____

_____

_____

# — Day 178 —

*"Do not strive for success blindly. You must have goals, a point you are aiming to reach."*

◄ *My Words of Success for Today* ►

_____

_____

_____

_____

_____

_____

_____

_____

_____

_____

# — Day 179 —

*"Some people just need to be pointed in the correct direction."*

◀ *My Words of Success for Today* ▶

_____

_____

_____

_____

_____

_____

_____

_____

_____

_____

## — Day 180 —

*"You need to ask yourself if the risk to achieve your goal is worth the potential consequences. If not, then take a step back, assess the situation, and find an alternative path to your success."*

_____

_____

_____

_____

_____

_____

_____

_____

_____

_____

# — Day 181 —

*"Never underestimate your goal."*

_____

_____

_____

_____

_____

_____

_____

_____

_____

# — Day 182 —

*"To deny Jesus is to reject your future
prosperity."*

◀ *My Words of Success for Today* ▶

_____

_____

_____

_____

_____

_____

_____

_____

_____

# — Day 183 —

*"Before you can reach for the future, you must first let go of what you are holding onto in the past."*

◀ *My Words of Success for Today* ▶

_____

_____

_____

_____

_____

_____

_____

_____

_____

# — Day 184 —

*"Success is largely dependent on the effort
put towards achieving it."*

◄ *My Words of Success for Today* ►

_____

_____

_____

_____

_____

_____

_____

_____

_____

_____

# — Day 185 —

*"Just because there is a path doesn't mean you should walk it."*

_____

_____

_____

_____

_____

_____

_____

_____

_____

# — Day 186 —

*"Every day learn at least one new word, and before long you will find that your vocabulary is significantly more impressive."*

_____

_____

_____

_____

_____

_____

_____

_____

_____

# — Day 187 —

*"If you see somebody in need, don't be afraid to stand up and help them. You might need their help someday."*

◂ *My Words of Success for Today* ▸

_____

_____

_____

_____

_____

_____

_____

_____

_____

# — Day 188 —

*"Seek to understand all that is around you so that you may succeed beyond what you thought possible."*

◄ *My Words of Success for Today* ►

_____

_____

_____

_____

_____

_____

_____

_____

_____

_____

# — Day 189 —

*"Success is usually achieved through many repeated efforts."*

*◄ My Words of Success for Today ►*

_____

_____

_____

_____

_____

_____

_____

_____

_____

# — Day 190 —

*"Stay on your path and under no circumstances let it be compromised by fallacies, doubts, or outward influences."*

◀ *My Words of Success for Today* ▶

_____

_____

_____

_____

_____

_____

_____

_____

_____

_____

# — Day 191 —

*"Move forward wisely. Others will be affected by your actions, too."*

_____

_____

_____

_____

_____

_____

_____

_____

_____

# — Day 192 —

*"There is no problem that doesn't have a solution. It is up to you to find that solution."*

_____

_____

_____

_____

_____

_____

_____

_____

_____

# — Day 193 —

*"You have three very simple choices in life. Move backward, stand still, or move forward. The time to make that choice is now."*

_____

_____

_____

_____

_____

_____

_____

_____

_____

_____

# — Day 194 —

*"Your knowledge is only limited by how much you're willing to learn."*

◀ *My Words of Success for Today* ▶

_____

_____

_____

_____

_____

_____

_____

_____

_____

_____

# — Day 195 —

*"The ability to move past your failures is critical for success."*

◀ *My Words of Success for Today* ▶

_____

_____

_____

_____

_____

_____

_____

_____

_____

# — Day 196 —

*"If you do not like the way your life is
going, then you must be the one to make a
stand and change it."*

◄ *My Words of Success for Today* ►

_____

_____

_____

_____

_____

_____

_____

_____

_____

# — Day 197 —

*"There's a fine line between just wanting
more and that of greed."*

◄ *My Words of Success for Today* ►

_____

_____

_____

_____

_____

_____

_____

_____

_____

# — Day 198 —

*"If you only make excuses, then making excuses will be the only thing you're good at."*

◀ *My Words of Success for Today* ▶

_____

_____

_____

_____

_____

_____

_____

_____

_____

# — Day 199 —

*"Without a goal and an objective, you will be without direction."*

◁ *My Words of Success for Today* ▷

_____

_____

_____

_____

_____

_____

_____

_____

_____

_____

# — Day 200 —

*"Does failure at an attempt to succeed mean you have lost? No. It only shows that you have found one way not to succeed."*

_____

_____

_____

_____

_____

_____

_____

_____

_____

# — Day 201 —

*"There is always an alternative, whether it
is obvious or not."*

◁ *My Words of Success for Today* ▷

_____

_____

_____

_____

_____

_____

_____

_____

_____

_____

# — Day 202 —

*"You should always plan for the worst but hope for the best."*

◄ *My Words of Success for Today* ►

_____

_____

_____

_____

_____

_____

_____

_____

_____

_____

# — Day 203 —

*"Stand tall, know what your reasons are,
and never let anybody pull you from your
path."*

◀ *My Words of Success for Today* ▶

_____

_____

_____

_____

_____

_____

_____

_____

_____

# — Day 204 —

*"To not do your best is a failure in itself."*

◂ *My Words of Success for Today* ▸

_____

_____

_____

_____

_____

_____

_____

_____

_____

# — Day 205 —

*"Mistakes will be made. It's standing back up and dusting yourself off that reveals your inner strength."*

◄ *My Words of Success for Today* ►

_____

_____

_____

_____

_____

_____

_____

_____

_____

# — Day 206 —

*"Before you fight tooth and nail for something, make sure it's worth fighting for."*

◅ *My Words of Success for Today* ▻

_____

_____

_____

_____

_____

_____

_____

_____

_____

# — Day 207 —

*"If you want to live your dreams, then you must put forth the necessary effort to achieve them."*

◀ My Words of Success for Today ▶

_____

_____

_____

_____

_____

_____

_____

_____

_____

_____

# — Day 208 —

*"Work to do things for the right reason, and you will find the rewards to be far greater. Soon you will find that you won't have to work at doing things for the right reason; it will come naturally."*

_____

_____

_____

_____

_____

_____

_____

_____

_____

# — Day 209 —

*"Seek not answers, but rather, the truth."*

◄ *My Words of Success for Today* ►

_____

_____

_____

_____

_____

_____

_____

_____

_____

_____

# — Day 210 —

*"Always understand that success is not a measure of wealth or power. It is the measure of achieving your goals, your desires, and your dreams."*

◀ *My Words of Success for Today* ▶

_____

_____

_____

_____

_____

_____

_____

_____

_____

# — Day 211 —

*"Never lose hope, for you don't know what tomorrow may bring."*

_____

_____

_____

_____

_____

_____

_____

_____

_____

# — Day 212 —

*"True success comes through trusting in the Lord and His Word every day of your life."*

◀ *My Words of Success for Today* ▶

_____

_____

_____

_____

_____

_____

_____

_____

_____

# — Day 213 —

*"Watch where you step, for you never know whose toes might be there."*

◁ *My Words of Success for Today* ▷

_____

_____

_____

_____

_____

_____

_____

_____

_____

# — Day 214 —

*"Not attempting to reach for the highest level of success imaginable is a failure to do your best."*

◄ *My Words of Success for Today* ►

_____

_____

_____

_____

_____

_____

_____

_____

_____

_____

# — Day 215 —

*"Time is your most valuable resource;*
*don't let it go to waste."*

◄ *My Words of Success for Today* ►

_____

_____

_____

_____

_____

_____

_____

_____

_____

_____

# — Day 216 —

*"Being honest and trustworthy will take you farther than deceit and disloyalty."*

_____

_____

_____

_____

_____

_____

_____

_____

_____

_____

# — Day 217 —

*"Without knowledge, drive, or passion,
you will find success fleeting."*

◂ *My Words of Success for Today* ▸

_____

_____

_____

_____

_____

_____

_____

_____

_____

_____

# — Day 218 —

*"The first and most effective method of
teaching is to lead by example."*

◄ *My Words of Success for Today* ►

_____

_____

_____

_____

_____

_____

_____

_____

_____

# — Day 219 —

*"Offer support to the struggling, and they will aid you in your rise to success."*

◄ *My Words of Success for Today* ►

_____

_____

_____

_____

_____

_____

_____

_____

_____

# — Day 220 —

*"Once you begin dwelling in the past, you will find your progress in life will come to a standstill."*

_____

_____

_____

_____

_____

_____

_____

_____

_____

_____

# — Day 221 —

*"Cross the line into greed, and you will always achieve less than you desire."*

◀ *My Words of Success for Today* ▶

_____

_____

_____

_____

_____

_____

_____

_____

_____

_____

## — Day 222 —

*"To truly be successful you must not only take responsibility for your actions but accept them willingly, whether they are positive or negative."*

_____

_____

_____

_____

_____

_____

_____

_____

_____

# — Day 223 —

*"When you are without a path, success
will escape your grasp."*

_____

_____

_____

_____

_____

_____

_____

_____

_____

_____

# — Day 224 —

*"Step back, observe what went wrong, and make another attempt. Learn this and you can reach your goal."*

◀ *My Words of Success for Today* ▶

_____

_____

_____

_____

_____

_____

_____

_____

_____

_____

# — Day 225 —

*"Opportunities may slip away. Always be watchful for the next one."*

*◀ My Words of Success for Today ▶*

_____

_____

_____

_____

_____

_____

_____

_____

_____

# — Day 226 —

*"Your words will open and close*
*opportunities in your life."*

◄ *My Words of Success for Today* ►

_____

_____

_____

_____

_____

_____

_____

_____

_____

## — Day 227 —

*"Understand the possibilities, know the consequences, yet don't give in to fear, or your progress will be nil."*

◄ *My Words of Success for Today* ►

_____

_____

_____

_____

_____

_____

_____

_____

_____

_____

# — Day 228 —

*"Believing that something is possible is the first step toward making it a realization."*

_____

_____

_____

_____

_____

_____

_____

_____

_____

_____

# — Day 229 —

*"Often failure is not a lack of knowledge,
but rather a lack of understanding."*

◂ *My Words of Success for Today* ▸

_____

_____

_____

_____

_____

_____

_____

_____

_____

# — Day 230 —

*"Understanding the obstacles in your life will allow you to overcome the negative effects that the fears, the opposition, and those who would stand against you have upon your life."*

_____

_____

_____

_____

_____

_____

_____

_____

_____

# — Day 231 —

*"The greatest understanding in the world comes not from knowledge, but from comprehension."*

◄ *My Words of Success for Today* ►

_____

_____

_____

_____

_____

_____

_____

_____

_____

_____

# — Day 232 —

*"Your success in life is not so much
dependent on your intelligence as it is on
the passion and effort you are willing to
put forward to achieve your goals."*

_____

_____

_____

_____

_____

_____

_____

_____

_____

# — Day 233 —

*"Success can often include wealth, power, and influence, but that's not the case for everyone."*

◀ *My Words of Success for Today* ▶

_____

_____

_____

_____

_____

_____

_____

_____

_____

_____

# — Day 234 —

*"Search for what you desire, be thankful for what you have, and work for what you need."*

*◄ My Words of Success for Today ►*

_____

_____

_____

_____

_____

_____

_____

_____

_____

# — Day 235 —

*"Everything you really need is within your grasp."*

◁ *My Words of Success for Today* ▷

_____

_____

_____

_____

_____

_____

_____

_____

_____

_____

# — Day 236 —

*"Acquiring what you desire is not a prerequisite to happiness."*

◂ *My Words of Success for Today* ▸

_____

_____

_____

_____

_____

_____

_____

_____

_____

# — Day 237 —

*"The process of achieving what you desire can bring you joy."*

◀ *My Words of Success for Today* ▶

_____

_____

_____

_____

_____

_____

_____

_____

_____

# — Day 238 —

*"When the core of who you are suffers to further wealth or power, then success has escaped you."*

◁ *My Words of Success for Today* ▷

_____

_____

_____

_____

_____

_____

_____

_____

_____

# — Day 239 —

*"Just because somebody knows the 'right' things to do in life, does not mean they will act on them."*

◀ *My Words of Success for Today* ▶

_____

_____

_____

_____

_____

_____

_____

_____

_____

# — Day 240 —

*"Live your life for what you want to be."*

◄ *My Words of Success for Today* ►

_____

_____

_____

_____

_____

_____

_____

_____

_____

# — Day 241 —

*"The deeper you dig your hole, the harder it is to climb out. Honesty is our ladder to success."*

◂ *My Words of Success for Today* ▸

_____

_____

_____

_____

_____

_____

_____

_____

_____

# — Day 242 —

*"Undertaking a decision without understanding the consequences of your action is a risky proposition."*

◀ *My Words of Success for Today* ▶

_____

_____

_____

_____

_____

_____

_____

_____

_____

# — Day 243 —

*"The more you improve your knowledge, the greater the value and number of opportunities that will become available to you."*

◄ *My Words of Success for Today* ►

_____

_____

_____

_____

_____

_____

_____

_____

_____

# — Day 244 —

*"Your mind is the greatest resource that you can own."*

◀ *My Words of Success for Today* ▶

_____

_____

_____

_____

_____

_____

_____

_____

_____

_____

# — Day 245 —

*"Standing up and doing what needs to be done is the only way you can truly make a difference."*

◂ *My Words of Success for Today* ▸

---

---

---

---

---

---

---

---

---

# — Day 246 —

*"Do not fear the unknown; once in a while
it will bring you a good surprise."*

◀ *My Words of Success for Today* ▶

_____

_____

_____

_____

_____

_____

_____

_____

_____

_____

# — Day 247 —

*"The easy path grants minimal rewards."*

◄ *My Words of Success for Today* ►

_____

_____

_____

_____

_____

_____

_____

_____

_____

# — Day 248 —

*"Do you doubt the words of those near you? Can you trust the people you associate with? You become like the people you spend time with."*

◄ *My Words of Success for Today* ►

_____

_____

_____

_____

_____

_____

_____

_____

_____

# — Day 249 —

*"Wisdom and patience go hand-in-hand with success."*

◄ *My Words of Success for Today* ►

_____

_____

_____

_____

_____

_____

_____

_____

_____

# — Day 250 —

*"You may feel overworked, but success
comes with determination."*

◀ *My Words of Success for Today* ▶

_____

_____

_____

_____

_____

_____

_____

_____

_____

_____

## — Day 251 —

*"Watch out for the agendas and desires of others. The path to your success is your responsibility."*

◄ *My Words of Success for Today* ►

_____

_____

_____

_____

_____

_____

_____

_____

_____

_____

# — Day 252 —

*"Step into the possibilities that come your way and don't allow them to go unused."*

⊲ *My Words of Success for Today* ⊳

_____

_____

_____

_____

_____

_____

_____

_____

_____

_____

# — Day 253 —

*"Watch for and understand the potential consequences of your words. Even a harmless comment or a small quip can do great damage."*

◁ *My Words of Success for Today* ▷

_____

_____

_____

_____

_____

_____

_____

_____

_____

_____

# — Day 254 —

*"Stand by what you know, hold your ground with the facts; do not be drawn away from the truths in your life."*

◀ *My Words of Success for Today* ▶

_____

_____

_____

_____

_____

_____

_____

_____

_____

# — Day 255 —

*"If you are doing something that would feel shameful if it were to become public, then it's probably something you shouldn't be doing."*

_____

_____

_____

_____

_____

_____

_____

_____

_____

# — Day 256 —

*"No obstacle is too great to overcome, but you must ask yourself if the cost to overcome the obstacle is worth the price."*

◀ *My Words of Success for Today* ▶

_____

_____

_____

_____

_____

_____

_____

_____

_____

_____

## — Day 257 —

*"Knowing what you're up against will
allow you to unpin yourself from the wall
of deceit, failure, restraint, and fear."*

◄ *My Words of Success for Today* ►

_____

_____

_____

_____

_____

_____

_____

_____

_____

# — Day 258 —

*"Knowing the why can be just as important as understanding the how."*

◄ *My Words of Success for Today* ►

_____

_____

_____

_____

_____

_____

_____

_____

_____

# — Day 259 —

*"Live out your own definition of success—*
*not somebody else's."*

◁ *My Words of Success for Today* ▷

_____

_____

_____

_____

_____

_____

_____

_____

_____

# — Day 260 —

*"If an opportunity comes your way, you
must take it and use it immediately."*

◄ *My Words of Success for Today* ►

_____

_____

_____

_____

_____

_____

_____

_____

_____

# — Day 261 —

*"Avoid the things that would divert you from your goal, for they will only become obstacles on your path to success."*

◀ *My Words of Success for Today* ▶

_____

_____

_____

_____

_____

_____

_____

_____

_____

# — Day 262 —

*"Never head into a situation with the attitude, 'I'm going to try.' Always enter a situation with, 'I will succeed.' "*

_____

_____

_____

_____

_____

_____

_____

_____

_____

# — Day 263 —

*"Investments are like water. If you leave them exposed, they will evaporate."*

◀ *My Words of Success for Today* ▶

_____

_____

_____

_____

_____

_____

_____

_____

_____

# — Day 264 —

*"Do not survive only by what is given to you. Reach out and achieve your desires."*

◄ *My Words of Success for Today* ►

_____

_____

_____

_____

_____

_____

_____

_____

_____

# — Day 265 —

*"Don't expect to achieve your goal if you're not willing to work towards it."*

◁ *My Words of Success for Today* ▷

_____

_____

_____

_____

_____

_____

_____

_____

_____

_____

# — Day 266 —

*"When you step on the course for success,*
*your path will carry you to your goal."*

_____

_____

_____

_____

_____

_____

_____

_____

_____

# — Day 267 —

*"Determine not just to expand your knowledge but to better understand the knowledge you already have."*

◂ *My Words of Success for Today* ▸

_____

_____

_____

_____

_____

_____

_____

_____

_____

# — Day 268 —

*"Success that harms your personal life,*
*your family, or your spirituality in the*
*guise of chasing money isn't true success."*

◄ *My Words of Success for Today* ►

_____

_____

_____

_____

_____

_____

_____

_____

_____

_____

# — Day 269 —

*"You have two paths before you. The
arduous one over the mountain provides
great rewards, or the short and easy path
gives minimal rewards. Which do you
choose?"*

_____

_____

_____

_____

_____

_____

_____

_____

_____

_____

# — Day 270 —

*"The act of betrayal can be agonizing and is one of the worst possible feelings. True success accompanies sincerity, truth, and loyalty."*

◀ *My Words of Success for Today* ▶

_____

_____

_____

_____

_____

_____

_____

_____

_____

_____

# — Day 271 —

*"The one who waits, the one with patience,*
*often receives the greatest reward."*

◁ *My Words of Success for Today* ▷

_____

_____

_____

_____

_____

_____

_____

_____

_____

# — Day 272 —

*"Your path may seem to be fading right in front of your eyes while everything slips from your grasp. Rather than give up, refocus on your goals."*

◁ *My Words of Success for Today* ▷

_____

_____

_____

_____

_____

_____

_____

_____

_____

# — Day 273 —

*"Never forget to say thank you."*

*◄ My Words of Success for Today ►*

_____

_____

_____

_____

_____

_____

_____

_____

_____

_____

# — Day 274 —

*"If you are not careful, lazy people will
begin to influence your goals and
objectives."*

◄ *My Words of Success for Today* ►

_____

_____

_____

_____

_____

_____

_____

_____

_____

_____

# — Day 275 —

*"Stick to the path you have chosen and do not falter."*

◀ *My Words of Success for Today* ▶

_____

_____

_____

_____

_____

_____

_____

_____

_____

_____

# — Day 276 —

*"Be observant. You never know how long until your next opportunity will appear."*

_____

_____

_____

_____

_____

_____

_____

_____

_____

# — Day 277 —

*"Always be respectful towards those who come against you; they are often the ones who need it the most."*

◄ *My Words of Success for Today* ►

_____

_____

_____

_____

_____

_____

_____

_____

_____

_____

# — Day 278 —

*"Even if what you say seems innocuous right now, will it still be so harmless ten, twenty, or even thirty years from now? Choose your words carefully."*

◀ *My Words of Success for Today* ▶

_____

_____

_____

_____

_____

_____

_____

_____

_____

## — Day 279 —

*"If you really want something, then you must attempt every possible avenue of success that is morally acceptable, no matter how exhausting, humiliating, or unpleasant it may be."*

◁ *My Words of Success for Today* ▷

_____

_____

_____

_____

_____

_____

_____

_____

_____

_____

# — Day 280 —

*"Know that the greatest obstacle in your path is none other than yourself."*

◀ *My Words of Success for Today* ▶

_____

_____

_____

_____

_____

_____

_____

_____

_____

# — Day 281 —

*"If you're only going to 'try' to do something, then you've already committed yourself to the eventual failure of reaching your potential."*

◄ *My Words of Success for Today* ►

_____

_____

_____

_____

_____

_____

_____

_____

_____

# — Day 282 —

*"Time can never be recovered. Once you've lost it, it's gone forever."*

◀ *My Words of Success for Today* ▶

---

---

---

---

---

---

---

---

---

# — Day 283 —

*"Without forgiveness, there is no future."*

*◄ My Words of Success for Today ►*

_____

_____

_____

_____

_____

_____

_____

_____

_____

_____

# — Day 284 —

*"Clearing out the logjam in front of you grants you the rightly deserved chance to truly shine, to unlock your full potential, to be able to encounter any obstacles and have the ability to not only overcome, but to learn from the encounter."*

_____

_____

_____

_____

_____

_____

_____

_____

_____

_____

# — Day 285 —

*"Stepping outside your current situation will teach you and give greater understanding of what you are facing."*

◄ *My Words of Success for Today* ►

_____

_____

_____

_____

_____

_____

_____

_____

_____

_____

# — Day 286 —

*"Doing something for the wrong reason
and doing something for the right reason
are two different paths to the same goal.
One will reap far greater benefits from
your actions."*

_____

_____

_____

_____

_____

_____

_____

_____

_____

# — Day 287 —

*"There is always a solution to your problem. You just have to find it."*

◄ *My Words of Success for Today* ►

_____

_____

_____

_____

_____

_____

_____

_____

_____

_____

# — Day 288 —

*"Trying something new is paramount for success."*

◀ *My Words of Success for Today* ▶

_____

_____

_____

_____

_____

_____

_____

_____

_____

_____

# — Day 289 —

*"Refuse to innovate and you'll find that you've been sitting still while the world passed you by."*

◀ *My Words of Success for Today* ▶

_____

_____

_____

_____

_____

_____

_____

_____

_____

_____

# — Day 290 —

*"If you strive to achieve only what you need, then you are existing only to survive."*

*◁ My Words of Success for Today ▷*

_____

_____

_____

_____

_____

_____

_____

_____

_____

# — Day 291 —

*"Do not limit yourself."*

◂ *My Words of Success for Today* ▸

_____

_____

_____

_____

_____

_____

_____

_____

_____

_____

# — Day 292 —

*"Once you let an opportunity pass you by,
it may be gone forever."*

◀ *My Words of Success for Today* ▶

---

---

---

---

---

---

---

---

---

---

# — Day 293 —

*"If you are at peace with yourself, you will
be at peace with all others."*

◁ *My Words of Success for Today* ▷

_____

_____

_____

_____

_____

_____

_____

_____

_____

_____

# — Day 294 —

*"Seek to understand that which you do not know, for knowledge stewards success."*

◄ *My Words of Success for Today* ►

_____

_____

_____

_____

_____

_____

_____

_____

_____

_____

# — Day 295 —

*"To be successful in all aspects of life,
you'll need people's help along the way."*

◄ *My Words of Success for Today* ►

_____

_____

_____

_____

_____

_____

_____

_____

_____

_____

# — Day 296 —

*"Never compromise on your moral grounds."*

◄ *My Words of Success for Today* ►

_____

_____

_____

_____

_____

_____

_____

_____

_____

# — Day 297 —

*"Stand firm and have unwavering resolve
to make a difference in the world."*

◄ *My Words of Success for Today* ►

_____

_____

_____

_____

_____

_____

_____

_____

_____

_____

# — Day 298 —

*"Listen to the words of the wise, for they often contain great insight."*

◀ *My Words of Success for Today* ▶

_____

_____

_____

_____

_____

_____

_____

_____

_____

_____

# — Day 299 —

*"If you see somebody in need, don't be afraid to help them."*

◀ *My Words of Success for Today* ▶

_____

_____

_____

_____

_____

_____

_____

_____

_____

_____

# — Day 300 —

*"Learning from a mistake is a success in its own right."*

*◀ My Words of Success for Today ▶*

_____

_____

_____

_____

_____

_____

_____

_____

_____

# — Day 301 —

*"Knowing and understanding the obstacles in your path will enable you to overcome the opposition you face."*

◀ *My Words of Success for Today* ▶

_____

_____

_____

_____

_____

_____

_____

_____

_____

# — Day 302 —

*"It only takes one step each day to begin
the process of achieving your goals."*

◀ *My Words of Success for Today* ▶

_____

_____

_____

_____

_____

_____

_____

_____

_____

_____

# — Day 303 —

*"Just because something seems
insurmountable does not mean that it is."*

◄ *My Words of Success for Today* ►

_____

_____

_____

_____

_____

_____

_____

_____

_____

_____

# — Day 304 —

*"A mind filled with knowledge is your key to success."*

_____

_____

_____

_____

_____

_____

_____

_____

_____

_____

# — Day 305 —

*"Selfishness and greed often go hand-in-hand with each other; if you spot one, then the other will soon join you."*

_____

_____

_____

_____

_____

_____

_____

_____

_____

_____

# — Day 306 —

*"You can either worry . . . or you can trust
God . . . but you CAN'T do both."*

◀ *My Words of Success for Today* ▶

_____

_____

_____

_____

_____

_____

_____

_____

_____

# — Day 307 —

*"If you want to achieve your goals, to reach out and surpass the impossible; then you must believe that it is not only possible, but that YOU can reach out and succeed."*

◁ *My Words of Success for Today* ▷

_____

_____

_____

_____

_____

_____

_____

_____

_____

# — Day 308 —

*"The only way to truly fail is to not even try."*

◄ *My Words of Success for Today* ►

_____

_____

_____

_____

_____

_____

_____

_____

_____

_____

# — Day 309 —

*"Wisdom is knowing the time to interfere."*

．

_____

_____

_____

_____

_____

_____

_____

_____

_____

_____

# — Day 310 —

*"Too early or too late and your opportunity will be gone."*

_____

_____

_____

_____

_____

_____

_____

_____

_____

# — Day 311 —

*"You may even feel lost, hopeless, and completely out of control while your every achievement and gain is torn from you. Remember, that's not who you are."*

◀ *My Words of Success for Today* ▶

_____

_____

_____

_____

_____

_____

_____

_____

_____

_____

# — Day 312 —

*"There is still hope. You just need to take that first step toward rectifying your problematic situation."*

◁ *My Words of Success for Today* ▷

_____

_____

_____

_____

_____

_____

_____

_____

_____

_____

# — Day 313 —

*"Being thankful for the things you have
and the assistance people have offered
will further your path to success."*

◄ *My Words of Success for Today* ►

_____

_____

_____

_____

_____

_____

_____

_____

_____

_____

# — Day 314 —

*"Your reach will be unfettered once you overcome your own inhibitions to success."*

◄ *My Words of Success for Today* ►

_____

_____

_____

_____

_____

_____

_____

_____

_____

# — Day 315 —

*"Your actions toward success speak louder
than your wishful thinking."*

◄ *My Words of Success for Today* ►

_____

_____

_____

_____

_____

_____

_____

_____

_____

# — Day 316 —

*"The actions and the consequences of those you associate with will reverberate throughout the lives of everyone near them."*

◀ *My Words of Success for Today* ▶

_____

_____

_____

_____

_____

_____

_____

_____

_____

_____

# — Day 317 —

*"Power is relative to the opposition it faces."*

◀ *My Words of Success for Today* ▶

_____

_____

_____

_____

_____

_____

_____

_____

_____

# — Day 318 —

*"Try at least one new thing every single day."*

*◀ My Words of Success for Today ▶*

_____

_____

_____

_____

_____

_____

_____

_____

_____

# — Day 319 —

*"Make the effort to bring your dreams, your needs, and the goals that extend far beyond just the necessities into reality."*

◄ *My Words of Success for Today* ►

_____

_____

_____

_____

_____

_____

_____

_____

_____

_____

# — Day 320 —

*"Assist those in need, and that assistance
will be repaid."*

◄ *My Words of Success for Today* ►

_____

_____

_____

_____

_____

_____

_____

_____

_____

# — Day 321 —

*"Success and hard work go hand-in-hand;*
*it's not something to be achieved easily."*

◂ *My Words of Success for Today* ▸

_____

_____

_____

_____

_____

_____

_____

_____

_____

_____

# — Day 322 —

*"Action changes lives."*

◄ *My Words of Success for Today* ►

_____

_____

_____

_____

_____

_____

_____

_____

_____

# — Day 323 —

*"There is a difference between dreaming of a better life and living it."*

_____

_____

_____

_____

_____

_____

_____

_____

_____

_____

# — Day 324 —

*"If there are multiple paths to the same goal, choose the one that is correct for your skillset."*

_____

_____

_____

_____

_____

_____

_____

_____

_____

_____

# — Day 325 —

*"Do what's right even when you don't have to. It will change your life for the better."*

⊲ *My Words of Success for Today* ⊳

_____

_____

_____

_____

_____

_____

_____

_____

_____

_____

# — Day 326 —

*"Giving your best when you don't feel like it motivates others to do the same."*

◀ *My Words of Success for Today* ▶

_____

_____

_____

_____

_____

_____

_____

_____

_____

_____

# — Day 327 —

*"How successful you've been isn't measured by where you are in life but instead by how far you've come."*

◁ *My Words of Success for Today* ▷

_____

_____

_____

_____

_____

_____

_____

_____

_____

_____

# — Day 328 —

*"Have faith and perseverance in pursuit of the success you are truly capable of achieving!"*

◀ *My Words of Success for Today* ▶

_____

_____

_____

_____

_____

_____

_____

_____

_____

_____

# — Day 329 —

*"If you are embarrassed to stand by what you've done, then a change is in order."*

◄ *My Words of Success for Today* ►

_____

_____

_____

_____

_____

_____

_____

_____

_____

# — Day 330 —

*"If it doesn't challenge you, it won't change you."*

◁ *My Words of Success for Today* ▷

_____

_____

_____

_____

_____

_____

_____

_____

_____

# — Day 331 —

*"Opportunities will come knocking on your door many times during your life, but if you don't greet and utilize them, success will not be yours."*

◄ *My Words of Success for Today* ►

_____

_____

_____

_____

_____

_____

_____

_____

_____

# — Day 332 —

*"Overcome all that stands in your path,
achieve success, and live a life that is
honorable and true."*

◁ *My Words of Success for Today* ▷

_____

_____

_____

_____

_____

_____

_____

_____

_____

# — Day 333 —

*"Admirable goals are worth the work to accomplish."*

◄ *My Words of Success for Today* ►

_____

_____

_____

_____

_____

_____

_____

_____

_____

_____

# — Day 334 —

*"Stepping back will give perspective and a superior understanding of what has happened and of what is to come, allowing you to make purposeful decisions."*

◄ *My Words of Success for Today* ►

_____

_____

_____

_____

_____

_____

_____

_____

_____

_____

# — Day 335 —

*"The ruler of success measures our progress from our start point, not from our present location."*

◂ *My Words of Success for Today* ▸

_____

_____

_____

_____

_____

_____

_____

_____

_____

_____

# — Day 336 —

*"Just because you've set a goal to achieve doesn't mean it will come easily."*

◄ *My Words of Success for Today* ►

_____

_____

_____

_____

_____

_____

_____

_____

_____

_____

# — Day 337 —

*"In the face of losing everything, you learn
what's important in your life."*

◄ *My Words of Success for Today* ►

_____

_____

_____

_____

_____

_____

_____

_____

_____

_____

# — Day 338 —

*"The word 'impossible' is just an excuse to not achieve success."*

*◁ My Words of Success for Today ▷*

_____

_____

_____

_____

_____

_____

_____

_____

_____

# — Day 339 —

*"Fear can't be your focus. You need to overcome your fear and not let it hinder your progress in life."*

◀ *My Words of Success for Today* ▶

_____

_____

_____

_____

_____

_____

_____

_____

_____

_____

# — Day 340 —

*"Complete success can be achieved only
by being accountable for your actions."*

◀ *My Words of Success for Today* ▶

_____

_____

_____

_____

_____

_____

_____

_____

_____

_____

# — Day 341 —

*"Until you have been brought low, you can never truly appreciate what it is to be raised high."*

_____

_____

_____

_____

_____

_____

_____

_____

_____

# — Day 342 —

*"You have the gift of choice. You must
choose to live a life of success."*

◀ *My Words of Success for Today* ▶

_____

_____

_____

_____

_____

_____

_____

_____

_____

# — Day 343 —

*"Want to know what's most important to you in life? Take a hard look at what you spend the majority of your time doing."*

◂ *My Words of Success for Today* ▸

_____

_____

_____

_____

_____

_____

_____

_____

_____

# — Day 344 —

*"If you find achieving your goal is becoming difficult, DON'T STOP! It just means you are moving closer to the summit of success!"*

*◁ My Words of Success for Today ▷*

_____

_____

_____

_____

_____

_____

_____

_____

_____

_____

# — Day 345 —

*"There are no perfect conditions, only perfect opportunities."*

◁ *My Words of Success for Today* ▷

_____

_____

_____

_____

_____

_____

_____

_____

_____

_____

# — Day 346 —

*"You have not failed unless you give up.
Continue onward . . . persist . . . don't stop
. . . for your success may be around the
next corner."*

◀ *My Words of Success for Today* ▶

_____

_____

_____

_____

_____

_____

_____

_____

_____

# — Day 347 —

*"Something is only impossible for as long as you believe it cannot be done."*

◀ *My Words of Success for Today* ▶

_____

_____

_____

_____

_____

_____

_____

_____

_____

_____

# — Day 348 —

*"The greatest success in life is
accomplishing the will of God."*

◀ *My Words of Success for Today* ▶

_____

_____

_____

_____

_____

_____

_____

_____

_____

_____

# — Day 349 —

*"Climbing a mountain is often hardest just before you reach the peak. You're nearly there!"*

◀ *My Words of Success for Today* ▶

_____

_____

_____

_____

_____

_____

_____

_____

_____

_____

# — Day 350 —

*"A lack of interest is to failure, as perseverance is to success."*

◀ *My Words of Success for Today* ▶

_____

_____

_____

_____

_____

_____

_____

_____

_____

_____

# — Day 351 —

*"Kind words said today create opportunities for tomorrow."*

◂ *My Words of Success for Today* ▸

_____

_____

_____

_____

_____

_____

_____

_____

_____

_____

# — Day 352 —

*"The rocks in our way can become*
*building blocks for our future."*

◀ *My Words of Success for Today* ▶

_____

_____

_____

_____

_____

_____

_____

_____

_____

# — Day 353 —

*"Stand straight, stand tall; don't fear those that would challenge you."*

◅ *My Words of Success for Today* ▻

_____

_____

_____

_____

_____

_____

_____

_____

_____

# — Day 354 —

*"The people to look up to are those who are already successful."*

◂ *My Words of Success for Today* ▸

_____

_____

_____

_____

_____

_____

_____

_____

_____

# — Day 355 —

*"What are you afraid of? Someone has
already conquered it. You can do it, too!"*

◀ *My Words of Success for Today* ▶

_____

_____

_____

_____

_____

_____

_____

_____

_____

_____

# — Day 356 —

*"When you stumble, check to see if the object in your way looks like you."*

_____

_____

_____

_____

_____

_____

_____

_____

_____

# — Day 357 —

*"Sometimes people won't hear your voice*
*because of all the things you do."*

◄ *My Words of Success for Today* ►

_____

_____

_____

_____

_____

_____

_____

_____

_____

# — Day 358 —

*"Preparation is your decision to become successful."*

◀ *My Words of Success for Today* ▶

_____

_____

_____

_____

_____

_____

_____

_____

_____

_____

# — Day 359 —

*"Each tick of the clock is a second of your life gone. Get busy now!"*

◀ *My Words of Success for Today* ▶

_____

_____

_____

_____

_____

_____

_____

_____

_____

# — Day 360 —

*"How you fill your day tells what you want out of your life."*

◀ *My Words of Success for Today* ▶

_____

_____

_____

_____

_____

_____

_____

_____

_____

_____

# — Day 361 —

*"If your goal isn't out of your comfort zone, you need to think bigger."*

◁ *My Words of Success for Today* ▷

_____

_____

_____

_____

_____

_____

_____

_____

_____

# — Day 362 —

*"Yesterday is a closed door. Look forward to find today's success."*

◀ *My Words of Success for Today* ▶

_____

_____

_____

_____

_____

_____

_____

_____

_____

# — Day 363 —

*"Look in the mirror to find your problem solver. It's up to you to change what you don't like."*

_____

_____

_____

_____

_____

_____

_____

_____

_____

# — Day 364 —

*"Put both hands on the handlebars. It's the only way to stay out of the ditch."*

◀ *My Words of Success for Today* ▶

_____

_____

_____

_____

_____

_____

_____

_____

_____

# — Day 365 —

*"If your year hasn't been successful, what are YOU going to do about it?"*

◀ *My Words of Success for Today* ▶

_____

_____

_____

_____

_____

_____

_____

_____

_____

www.ingramcontent.com/pod-product-compliance
Lightning Source LLC
Chambersburg PA
CBHW060240100426

42742CB00011B/1587